Nile Wilson

Raising the Bar

Nile Wilson
Raising the Bar

How Gymnastics can
Change your Life

WHITE OWL
AN IMPRINT OF PEN & SWORD BOOKS LTD.
YORKSHIRE – PHILADELPHIA

First published in Great Britain in 2018 by
Pen and Sword White Owl
An imprint of Pen and Sword Books
Pen & Sword Books Ltd.
Yorkshire – Philadelphia

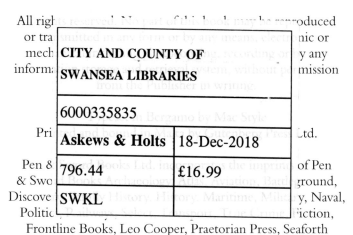

Printed and bound in England by CPI Group (UK) Ltd., Croydon, CR0 4YY

Pen & Sword Books Ltd. incorporates the imprints of Pen
& Sword Books Archaeology, Atlas, Aviation, Battleground,
Discovery, Family History, History, Maritime, Military, Naval,
Politics, Railways, Select, Transport, True Crime, Fiction,
Frontline Books, Leo Cooper, Praetorian Press, Seaforth
Publishing, Wharncliffe and White Owl.

For a complete list of Pen & Sword titles please contact

PEN & SWORD BOOKS LIMITED
47 Church Street, Barnsley, South Yorkshire, S70 2AS, England
E-mail: enquiries@pen-and-sword.co.uk
Website: www.pen-and-sword.co.uk

or

PEN AND SWORD BOOKS
1950 Lawrence Rd, Havertown, PA 19083, USA
E-mail: Uspen-and-sword@casematepublishers.com
Website: www.penandswordbooks.com

Contents

One

Why Gymnastics can Change your Life!

Since the age of four, gymnastics has been my life. Sometimes it feels like my passion for the sport is quite literally bursting out and I want to share that with everyone I can!

I know gymnastics can change your life regardless of your age, shape or physical capability. There is something in it for everyone to love and enjoy. You can find achievement

and an enormous sense of pride through participating in the sport.

I respect and admire other sports, but gymnastics is unique in what it can offer you both physically and mentally. It becomes a way of life that teaches your mind and body disciplines that stay with you forever. It really doesn't matter what age you choose to join in, so whether you are five or fifty-five years old, I believe awesome things can happen to you through participating in my sport.

First and foremost, gymnastics is fun! We get to play and experiment on all sorts of brilliant equipment and call it 'training'. Gymnastics is the closest thing to human beings learning how to fly. Just by practising and developing our skills on a daily basis, we are improving our body and mind. And that's it; all you have to do with gymnastics is join in and realise all the benefits that come with it. That's a pretty good deal in my eyes.

I see people who trudge to the gym every day in search of that perfect body, perhaps one they have seen in a magazine,

or one that they have seen at the gym. They do the same exercises they've always done, staying within their comfort zone, and not really getting anywhere or even enjoying it. It doesn't have to be that way! Gymnastics can provide you with a different approach that will change how you feel about training, and a body change will develop through continued participation in the sport. I know that in order to drive a sustainable approach to training you have to change the way you feel about it, and in order to do that you have to drive a different belief. That can sometimes be a challenge; however, it can also be very easy.

I was lucky that my parents took me to try gymnastics at a very young age. I was a clumsy kid who loved climbing up everything, so Mum and Dad thought a gymnasium was the safest place for me. My mum actually said it was an

opportunity for me to release some of my energy and learn how to fall. I fell in love with it immediately and had some natural physical ability for it as well. So much of what I am going to talk about in this book has been ingrained in me for many years; it has made my life and attitude what it is today and I truly believe it is available to everyone who wants it.

It is a sport that teaches you discipline, structure, routine and concentration. At eight years old, I was doing twenty-four hours a week in the gym, but I still completed all my homework on time. School was very important to me, and I made sure that I achieved as much as I could academically. However, I always longed to be in the gym to try the next move or strength challenge that I was aiming for.

Gymnastics teaches you how to perform as an individual and also how to appreciate the importance of the team, but most importantly, it can teach you how to overcome fear. I believe that so many people in life are held back by fear, whether it is fear of failure or fear of what people may think of you, and at its core, gymnastics teaches you to overcome that. I regard fear as an opportunity to learn and grow as a person. Overcoming fear has driven some of my best results in gymnastics as well as in life.

Learning a new skill in gymnastics can be one of the most exhilarating experiences. You are trying something that you're not sure you can physically do. Fear can consume you when you feel completely out of your comfort zone. That apprehension is a mindset that you can control, and this is something I will talk about later in the book. In moments of fear you can make a choice to go for it and commit yourself 100 per cent. Making that decision and then producing the skill is an amazing feeling. I have watched grown men learn to do a somersault for the first time and be buzzing about it for weeks afterwards. I have witnessed my dad overcome his fear to do a back somersault and be thoroughly exhilarated. The feelings he was experiencing were perhaps similar to those of flying a plane, hitting a hole in one in golf, or winning the lottery. He was buzzing about a somersault, in a controlled environment in the gym. You too can create those amazing feelings.

And what does this type of experience teach you for life away from the gymnasium? Everything! It helps you to believe in yourself. You have shown that if you commit to something 100 per cent, you can do it. And that's addictive.

You can recreate those feelings time and again by challenging yourself further and learning more skills. You can also take this attitude into your work and home life, relationships, and beyond. It's incredible!

As a gymnast you learn to listen to feedback and understand the importance for development. Gymnastics is a sport in which you quite literally get judged every time you perform a skill. You will immediately receive comments from a coach, and only for good reasons. This teaches you important lessons about how to absorb criticism in a positive manner. Receiving feedback is just as important, or possibly more important, than giving it to someone else. If you are prepared to listen to, digest and use the feedback to develop yourself then that has to be a good thing. How many people find hearing feedback a challenge at school, at home or in the workplace? Gymnastics provides a safe environment in which to regard feedback as something that will allow you to improve and grow.

This might sound strange, but gymnasts are used to failure. We make mistakes constantly, but that's OK, because we know it brings us one step closer to perfection. So we embrace the fact that we will make mistakes along the way, learning from the feedback and experience to help us improve. I know that I feel secure with the fact that I am always trying to do my very best in life, and that's all I can do. I measure myself against progress and not perfection, and this has helped me deal with setbacks because I have developed a coping mechanism in case everything doesn't go perfectly. In 2017, I suffered a major ankle injury, which was followed by reconstructive surgery. After the high of the 2016 Olympics I found myself sitting on the sofa wondering when I would get back to gymnastics, but not for a moment did I give up. I know that in times of difficulty I can't affect what has happened to me; I can only control my attitude towards it. Again, this is something I will return to later. I understand setbacks happen and I can quickly move forward from them. I set a plan and came back stronger than ever. This perspective has been borne partly from my life experiences and family values, but mainly from my training in gymnastics.

I have always seen gymnastics as an art. It taps into a creative part of my brain as I imagine what my body can do. And there are no limits. I love the fact that I can try a new skill every day I walk into the gym. Performing a new routine or skill is like painting a picture in my mind. I don't feel like a robot, I feel like an artist. Yes we have to practise routines but there is a beauty to it, and the key to this is that it is not exclusive to an Olympian. You can all do this in whatever you try in gymnastics. Compare this to trudging on the treadmill!

You may have noticed that up until now I have focused mainly on how gymnastics can help your mind. I have purposely started here because many people may initially consider that you need certain physical attributes in order to be able to perform gymnastics. Let's face it; we gymnasts have pretty decent bodies! But in some ways, the mind is the hidden secret of gymnastics. At Leeds Gymnastics Club, where I train, I watch the adult classes in the evening and talk to some of the people who participate. I can see the sparkle in their eyes from what gymnastics has brought to their lives. It has focused their mind and given them a release from the stresses of day-to-day life. That's why I want to share it with everyone.

Nonetheless, the physical benefits of gymnastics are massive and a good portion of this book will concentrate on that.

Gymnasts are in great physical shape, with incredible body composition and definition. An important point is that I have not got this body by looking in the mirror and hyperfocusing on improving one part of it. I have never wished for a six-pack or urged my biceps to get bigger; I have just developed this way by doing gymnastics every day of my life.

And that's it – gymnastics can help you improve your body by simply taking part. The reason for this is that every part of your body is worked. Let's just think about what doing a handstand does for your body. Of course, the main tension is in your shoulders, but at the same time your whole body is helping to maintain the position. Your hands create your base as every muscle and tendon in them helps to stabilise you. Likewise, your wrists and arms work like crazy to stop you from wobbling all over the place. Your shoulders are then in prime position to maintain this, but your neck and chest will be holding tight as well, helping to develop your core strength. Finally, your legs and feet can't just flop loosely. They have to do their part to hold strong and still. There isn't one part of your body taking it easy during a handstand. Your core is constantly being worked in gymnastics – it always works multiple muscle groups at the same time, which is referred to in the gym as 'compound' training. This boosts your heart rate and causes you to burn more calories.

Clearly gymnastics can be very physically demanding. It's part of the territory, especially if you want to reach the highest levels. But with more recreational gymnastics you can gear the physical demands to your own goals. It is you who is pushing your body so it is entirely up to you how hard you push. The beauty of gymnastics is that you are working against your body weight. You are not trying to lift obscene one-off weights in a gym; you are learning to hold, push and throw your own body weight.

I watch the four and five year olds enter our gym and start by learning the core body functions of balance, coordination and space awareness. It was the same for me when my parents first took me to the gym. Your body is learning how to control itself against its own weight. Learning these movements and

teaching your body to work in balance is invaluable at that age, or at any age for that matter.

'Improving your core' has become a fashionable thing heard in fitness gyms across the country. Core exercises train the muscles in your pelvis, lower back, hips and abdomen to work in harmony with each other. This leads to better balance and stability. There are specific classes that aim to improve these areas and can often help people with back problems caused by being slumped at a desk all day. My passion for the sport is often matched by a frustration that more adults are not already doing it for this very reason!

Flexibility is also a big part of gymnastics, and I will look at this in more detail in a later chapter. The benefits of remaining flexible are huge. Keeping your muscles long and lean helps prevent things like back problems. Stretching is an important part of every gymnastics session and the benefits will last a lifetime. By doing regular stretching exercises you also learn relaxation techniques and how to control your breathing. So many people enjoy yoga, and I can understand why, but the vehicle to improve your core strength and flexibility is waiting for you in your local gymnastics club!

Gymnastics becomes a way of life and can stay with you forever. It offers you a sustainable way of being healthy in mind and body. It's not a post-Christmas fad to make up for eating and drinking too much – it is so much more. I know that when I finish competing, I will maintain my physical shape and discipline because it is part of who I am. It helps me take on challenges from all aspects of life.

These are the reasons I want to share my enthusiasm for the sport with other people. Gymnastics isn't just about winning medals in competitions – it is about enhancing your life in all manner of ways. The greatest secret of gymnastics is… there is no secret!

Two

We can all have the Mindset of an Olympian

I believe there is a common misconception that Olympic athletes have been born with talent and a positive mindset that allows them to compete at the highest possible levels. That is just not true. Developing an incredible mindset towards sport, work and life in general is achievable by ALL of us.

I once read that when a baby is born they only have two things hardwired other than wanting to feed: fear of falling and fear of noises. Everything else is learnt behaviour. The mind is like any muscle in your body – it needs training and nurturing. I wouldn't walk out and try to perform in an Olympic final without having done enough physical training, so neither would I expect to have a great mindset without having worked on it consistently over a number of years.

It's probably worth us quickly looking at what we mean by 'mindset'. To me this means my attitude to life, not just gymnastics, and how I choose to deal mentally with all the good and difficult things life can throw at you. And it's very much a choice we can all make and a habit we can get into. It's just not true that some people are born with a better mindset than others. People with great attitudes to life have made a choice to have that perspective, and they work on it. Likewise, people with a bad attitude have also made a conscious or subconscious decision not to break out of it, and it has become a really negative habit in their life.

I'm going to take you through my five cornerstones to having a great mindset, but before I do that I want to draw from the incredible experience that the 2016 Rio Olympic Games was for me. I learnt so many lessons about achieving a good mindset during what were the greatest three weeks of my life so far.

The first thing to say about competing in a major event like the Olympic Games is that it is quite a long process. All in all, from qualification to the high bar final, it was two weeks for me, as that final was the very last event. Two weeks is a long time to maintain your focus, composure and relaxation.

I remember arriving at the Olympic Village and being surrounded by 20,000 other top athletes, some of whom were idols of mine, and I just couldn't stop smiling. The enormity

PA Images.

of the experience wasn't lost on me and I wanted to absorb every moment.

We began with the qualifications days as a team and as individuals. The team did brilliantly and we were in fourth place for the final, while I qualified in fifth for the all-around final. That meant I would begin on the floor as one of the top gymnasts to start on an apparatus. In fact, I very clearly remember the moment I was lining up on the floor with the other top six qualifiers in front of the judges. I was standing with the kings of gymnastics and it was an incredible feeling. But more importantly, I felt like I belonged there. It was exactly where I wanted to be. I was nervous, but I wasn't scared. I had worked all my life, both mentally and physically, for this and I wanted to be there more than anything else. I have heard of sports people freezing in that moment, but it wasn't like that for me. I am convinced this was because of my mental preparation, which had been going on for many years.

I went into the team and all-around final with the same attitude: let's just have fun and enjoy it. The team final was slightly different to the individual because I felt the pressure of not wanting to let down my teammates, but I still held on to the belief that this should be an enjoyable experience. And I performed some of the best gymnastics of my life. My score of 15.7 on the high bar was the highest in the competition, and I was able to carry this form into the all-around final. I nailed all six routines, finishing eighth at only twenty years old.

I then had six days before the high bar final, which was the very last event. Those six days felt like six years! It was so tough mentally because I had just come down from the adrenaline rush of the team and all-around finals, and I now needed to hold everything together to compete in a single discipline final.

PA Images.

A lot can go wrong mentally over six days; in fact, it is easier to think about all the things that can go wrong rather than things that can go right. Unfortunately, that's what we humans tend to do: you can burn too much nervous energy and become exhausted, or you can start to switch off and relax too much. You have to find a mental place where you can relax but stay in the moment of being at an Olympic Games getting ready to compete for medals.

I knew that the 6-day wait was completely out of my control. I had to accept it and adapt to it, and not spend any time stressing about it. I had a choice – I could choose to be scared, believing that I was out of my comfort zone, or I could choose to remember that I was at an Olympic Games, where I had wanted to be for so long, and just enjoy the whole process. Maintaining a positive mental attitude was a choice that I made, and that's something I will talk more about in this chapter.

By the time it came to my high bar final, Max Whitlock had won three medals, Louis Smith had won a medal and Bryony Page had won a trampolining medal. The list of medal winners that was hanging up outside of our apartment was getting longer and longer. There was a massive buzz around Team GB and I almost felt like it was expected that I would win a medal! And then Amy Tinkler won a bronze on the floor while I was waiting for my final to start. It definitely added to the pressure and I had to block that out. You can't put your hand into your pocket and pull out some pressure, or go into a shop and buy some pressure; in that situation pressure is a self-induced state, a state that you put yourself in. So I focused on the process, not the outcome. When it comes to the crux of performing in a massive final, it is all about process. You have done that routine a million times and you just have to do it one more time. I had never focused on the outcome or result previously, so why would I dwell on that now? Process, process, process!

But achieving that mindset takes practice. I'm an emotional person and tend to react to the energy of people around me, so it's not my natural way to block all of that out and concentrate on a simple process. This is something I have worked on for years.

With half an hour to go before the start of the final I was feeling a massive range of emotions. I was obviously very nervous, but knew that I only had one shot at it, so I thought, 'I might as well smash this!'

Having said that, I also remember that a year before the Olympics I had asked Louis Smith what it was like to compete in an Olympic final. His answer was, 'Nile, nothing will ever prepare you for what it feels like to compete in an Olympic final. Like ever.' And it wasn't until I stepped up onto the podium and stood by the chalk bucket that I understood exactly what he meant. The magnitude of that moment is crazy. It is true – nothing can you prepare for it. Nothing.

So how did I handle the intensity of that moment? I talked my way through it. Instead of allowing negative fears about what could go wrong to run through my head, I told myself that I could do this, and thought about what could go right. And I go back to my point about having fun. I also just wanted to enjoy myself out there.

When it came to the actual routine, I don't remember anything about it. My first memory is of my feet hitting the floor and sticking the dismount. It was like I was on autopilot. My body and mind had done this a million times and they were just doing exactly what I had prepared for. Preparation is the absolute key. Every time you think about the routine, you are preparing. You don't have to physically do it thousands of times, you just have to think about it, and the mind is mentally preparing you for that moment. You can't expect yourself to

suddenly develop a great mindset in the intensity of a moment like an Olympic final. It has to have been practised again and again, so that it just clicks in when you most need it. My mind and body were ready for that moment after sixteen years of preparation; and thankfully, it meant I won a bronze medal at my first Olympic Games.

I learnt so much from that experience and it reinforced for me the key things behind having a great mindset. These five points can help you to start improving your mindset from TODAY!

1. POSITIVE SELF-TALK

'No one succeeded their way to success' is one of my favourite sayings, and so true to my beliefs. As gymnasts, we are always looking to perfect our routines, which means we will mess them up many times in practice. We embrace failure. Many people in business I have spoken to say the same thing about the success of their businesses. They have made a ton of mistakes, but have learnt from them quickly. A mistake or failure is just a step closer to getting it right. Talking to yourself about this throughout the day is important.

My friend and mentor Michael Finnigan has done extensive research on how the brain works and how we talk to ourselves. The science is out there for anyone to research. Michael made me aware that scientists believe we talk to ourselves 50,000 times a day. I'm going to say that again… 50,000 TIMES A DAY! If most of the self-talk that goes on in your brain is negative – 'I can't', 'I won't', 'I don't like' – then it will affect your behaviour, and ultimately, your performance in whatever you are trying to achieve.

We all make mistakes, but if you tell yourself that you can do something, you will learn quickly and move forward. As I said in the previous chapter, every training session for me is a step out of my comfort zone, but I tell myself I can do it again and again. In every moment, in every training session, in every competition – 'I CAN DO THIS'.

Say that phrase to yourself every single day. Say it out loud and make it real, even if it doesn't come naturally at first. Just keep practising it. At the same time, start to become more aware of your thoughts. Do you have a lot of negative thoughts? If so, just being aware of that allows you to start to change them. Being self-aware is the first step in being able to make positive choices to improve your mindset. It starts with your belief – your self-belief will drive your attitude every time. My belief at the Olympics was that I was going to have fun and enjoy it. That's what drove my attitude and ultimately, my performance.

This is such a simple point and it is difficult for many people, but from today we can all start to talk to ourselves in a more positive manner. Practise it and make it a habit.

2. GOALS

Set yourself goals on a daily, weekly and monthly basis. Start with daily, bite-sized goals and work up from there.

I set myself a daily goal to improve a new skill I am working on in the gym. But that daily goal can relate to almost anything in someone's work, school or personal life. It could be to complete a work project, call a family member you haven't spoken to for ages, or do your best in a school test. The important point is that they are daily goals and they are achievable.

It is vital that goals are set so that your mind can help support you in what you're trying to achieve. If you do not set goals for yourself then you will continue to be the person you are today, and that is fine if you are where you want to be. If you want to improve then write your goals down and focus 100 per cent on achieving them. Keep on reading them out to yourself! Just remember – whatever your goals are, they will involve hard work. Don't just leave them on that piece of paper.

From there you can set yourself more medium and long-term targets, such as getting a promotion at work, losing a certain amount of weight or even winning an Olympic gold! But we need those smaller goals to drive ourselves forward in what we are doing. I often see people set themselves unrealistic goals and then get disheartened when it seems impossible to achieve them. So give yourself smaller stepping stones and gather momentum. With momentum comes confidence, and with that comes more positive self-talk and self-belief.

3. FIND FUN AND ENJOYMENT

We all have twenty-four hours in the day, but it is our choice how we use them.

You have to find fun and enjoyment in your life. Find your passion, whether it is in or outside of your work. I am extremely lucky that I absolutely love gymnastics and so going to the gym is not a chore for me. Actually, that's not true; sometimes I'm very sore and would prefer to lie in a hot tub, but you know what I mean – I love doing what I do.

I am lucky, but that doesn't mean this isn't available to everyone. Of course, many people choose to work in a job they don't love and it pays the bills. But this doesn't mean you can't search for fun outside of work. You have many more hours left in the day. Go and do something you love, whether it's playing 5-a-side football or a musical instrument, or painting, or seeing friends. Make the most of every day. It is a choice!

Just as the Olympics taught me, we achieve our best when we are having fun and doing it with a smile on our face.

4. CHOOSE YOUR ATTITUDE

The whole way through this chapter I have emphasised that improving your mindset is a choice that everyone can make.

I wake up every day and genuinely think, 'How can I be the best version of myself today?' That's a choice I make on how I want to handle my day. Whatever our background or circumstances, we all have that basic decision to make about our attitude for the day. Do we want to get dragged down by negativity, or do we choose to face the world positively? Do we choose to say to ourselves 'I am going to have great day because...' or do we say, 'Today is going to be a bad day because...'?

Part of choosing a good attitude is accepting that not everything will go perfectly every day. I might get caught in a traffic jam, but that doesn't have to define the rest of my day. How many people do you speak to who say, 'The traffic was horrendous; I can't stand that drive, it made me late!'? It's just a queue, yet we can make so much more of it, and that defines how we behave and what people think of us. If it makes you late, get up earlier! Accept, adapt and move on. Gymnasts are really good at this. If we make a mistake in the middle of a routine, we can't just give up on the competition. We hang in there, persevere and move forward. That's my attitude with life, and that's a choice.

An important memory for me in relation to this is the 2014 Junior European Championships in Sofia, Bulgaria. I qualified for the all-around final and felt that I was favourite to win. In 2012 I had won silver in the same competition behind my great friend, Frank Baines. My first piece in the final was the vault, in which I performed OK. I still felt great, but early in my next piece, the parallel bars, I sat on the bar during a move called the Tipelt. This cost me a mark and I found myself lying in thirteenth place after the second rotation. I clearly remember believing that I could still win. My attitude was that I could smash all of my next routines and still take gold. I did not want another silver medal. I was determined, focused, and most importantly, undeterred by my mistake on

the parallel bars. In the end I won gold, after following up the mistake with four of my best routines as a junior gymnast on the next pieces. It was a magic moment for me, and one I choose to remember well now.

I could have put myself in a place that would have affected the outcome in a different way; that mistake could have been my 'traffic jam' that affected the rest of my competition negatively. I didn't want that to happen. The power of my goal to win was far stronger than the obstacle that I had placed in the way through poor execution on a move.

Things will not always go your way and dealing with setbacks is part of what makes us who we are. Having a good mindset is very much in YOUR control!

5. VISUALISATION

I can sit here, close my eyes and think back to the Olympic Games. I can bring myself back to that very moment and get goosebumps doing so. The mind is so powerful and using visualisation can help prepare you for great things.

Allow your mind to dream great things and visualise yourself achieving the goals you have set yourself. Make them come alive in your mind. By doing this, you are preparing yourself for those achievements, and in turn making them more possible. Visualisation means that when a great moment happens, it will not be the first time you have been there in your mind. Again, it doesn't matter if this is within sport or your working or personal life.

I think back to that Olympic final when my mind and body slipped into autopilot. I knew I had the ability to get it right because I had done it a million times before. I had visualised being in that Olympic final many times over. Although it was the most intense experience, I was ready for it.

Visualisation needs practice though. It's not a switch you can turn on and off. You need time on your own, without your phone or other distractions, to practise letting your mind go.

Those are my five cornerstones to having a great mindset, and if you practise them on a daily basis, I truly believe that confidence will flood into your life. Make having a positive mindset a habit. It needs work and dedication, but it is so worth it. Just as negative thinking can be a self-defeating process, positive thinking can be self-fulfilling.

Three

Food

This chapter is not about me trying to portray myself as some sort of nutritional expert. I'm not. It is about me sharing my experiences, both good and bad, about food and nutrition. I am an Olympian, but I believe that I can offer insight that can help everyone.

I only really started to take nutrition seriously when I was fourteen or fifteen years old. Prior to that I pretty much ate what I wanted. As a family we would eat multiple takeaways a week and I loved my sweets and chocolate. I hated vegetables! I honestly never gave it a thought. I had been training hard since the age of five or six, so burning calories wasn't an issue for me. But as I was approaching my fifteenth birthday, British Gymnastics brought a nutritionist on board and she completely opened my eyes as to how I could improve my performance by eating better, and how bad my nutrition had been up to that point.

The advice was a catalyst for me to change, and within two months I lost 2 kilograms of fat, which for a fairly lean fifteen year old was a lot. Even more importantly, I also became English and British Champion, so I immediately saw the benefit of developing a better diet. To this day I recognise how important it is for me to have a good diet in order to be mentally and physically strong.

Only a year or so later, my focus around my diet had developed into something not necessarily healthy. I became obsessed with my weight rather than with how I felt. It started

when I began weighing myself every day. I was obsessed about how light I could get and was convinced that that would make me a better gymnast. I had conditioned myself to believe that the lighter I was, the more I could throw myself around in the gym. I ignored how I felt and just wanted the number on the weighing scales to be as low as possible.

I was sixteen years old and went from weighing 61 kilograms in January to 53 kilograms in May, when I was competing in the European Championships. At 61 kilograms I didn't need to lose any weight. I was already lean and strong, but I'd just got in this mental state of eating less and trying to become lighter and lighter. It was very unhealthy. I had become so consumed by that belief that I would not just eat the right food when I was hungry, but needed to check in detail the nutritional value of any food I was about to eat. Like any unhealthy obsession, it was controlling me rather than me controlling it.

Don't get me wrong; the moment I started to take my nutrition seriously was a game changer for me on a general performance level, but by this time it had developed into something different. I competed OK in the European Championships; I was part of the team that won gold and also won the individual all-around silver, but I missed out on a high bar medal having qualified well for the final. However, throughout the competition I felt weak and tired. My behaviour changed as well. I isolated myself and spent a lot of time away from the rest of the team. Anyone who knows me knows how unusual that is for me. I love being around people, but I didn't feel like that anymore. The experience made me realise the serious impact that my attitude to nutrition was having on my mental health and wellbeing. Having a good diet is about feeling physically *and* mentally healthy.

There's no question that there can be a real intensity around your weight as a gymnast. One kilo can make a big difference at the bottom of a swing or on the rings, or with your impact on the floor. When I was sixteen, I focused on the weight that the scales were showing me. It was all that seemed important, not how I felt, and that's a dangerous thing. I see many gymnasts weighing themselves morning and night, and it has a big impact on their mood. They train hard and yet can wake up the next day and find out they weigh more than the previous day, which can have a really negative influence on their focus for the rest of the day. Everything hangs on the number on the weighing scales.

This problem also had an impact on my family life. Strong family values are something that I am very passionate about, but during this period I would say no to quality family time, such as us all going out for a meal together, through fear of the impact that meal would have on me. While in Montpellier (a really beautiful place) for the European Championships, a simple walk down the coast to the harbour was something I didn't want to do as I was concerned about using energy. I felt like I didn't have much energy in the first place, so didn't want to waste it.

I actually steer clear of the weighing scales now so that I can avoid that cycle and rely more on how I feel. Obviously if you are trying to lose weight, then it is only natural to want to weigh yourself to check your progress, but don't hang

everything on it. Look in the mirror and go by how you feel. Do you feel strong, happy and healthy? If yes, then you are doing the right things. Chasing a number on the scales can become a dangerous cycle for an Olympian, or anyone just trying to be fitter and healthier.

The impact of that period of my life still lives with me today. The discipline and hyperfocus on what I ate created a flip side that is just as harmful – binge eating. I am a thousand times better at handling this now, but it is an issue I have to keep my eye on, even to this day. During this period there were times when I could eat brilliantly for weeks or months on end, but then really struggle to control myself and end up binge eating. Binge eating is not just someone over indulging who needs to control themselves; it is much more than that.

I want to explain how binge eating happens with me so that people can gain a better understanding of this sort of eating disorder. I could be extremely disciplined with my eating for a decent period of time, but I was like a pressure cooker building up. The focus on what I should and should not eat would be so intense that eventually I would blow. Once this happened I was not in control. Two or three hours could go by and I wouldn't really know what had happened. It would just be about me eating more and more and more. My stomach would be uncomfortably full having eaten four or five times more food than I needed to. It was far more serious than eating a bit too much chocolate or an extra bowl of ice cream; it was extreme eating, sometimes until 3.00 am. It was horrible.

Then the shame and massive guilt would hit: 'Why have I done this?' 'How did this happen?' It would have a hugely negative impact on the days that followed. I would try to solve the problem I had created for myself by hardly eating at all, and at the same time be training hard. Then the pressure cooker would be building up once more, and bang… it would happen again. I was back in a vicious cycle.

A lot of it would centre on the weekend, when things would go wrong. Monday, Tuesday and Wednesday would be average days in the gym after a binge. At times I could weigh 3 or 4 kilograms heavier than normal and might struggle to train properly. I would then wrestle things back towards the end of the week, before bingeing again at the weekend. And so the cycle would begin again: it was as if I was inside a spinning wheel and couldn't get out.

It became even more dangerous when I tried to keep everything secret. In the past I have got up at 1.00 am and eaten five bowls of cereal while my parents were asleep so they wouldn't know. It's a horrible place to be in and it just shows that I might be an Olympic athlete but, like many other people, I have had issues with food. I hope that the lessons I have learnt through dealing with all of this can be helpful to other people.

I have managed to drag myself out of the binge eating cycle over a period of time. There wasn't a moment when I just snapped out of it. It doesn't work like that. It just has to get better steadily and I now feel much more in control.

Here are some key things that helped me overcome my eating problem:

➡ **Being open about it to family and friends.** Telling my parents the full extent of my issues has been enormously important to me. Of course they support me regardless, but if they don't know about how bad a problem is then they don't necessarily know what they need to do to help. I'm really open about it all now, as I am in this book, because it genuinely helps me to hear it said out loud. Telling people whom you trust and who care about you is so important, but so is telling people who understand. People who don't have these sorts of difficulties with food might find the problem hard to relate to, so look for people who do understand how horrible it is.

➥ **A little bit of something naughty to eat is not bad!** I don't deny myself eating something a bit naughty from time to time. The odd bit of chocolate is absolutely fine so I don't beat myself up about it. I think that's the key; previously I would feel bad for eating something a little bit naughty and then overreact. Now I just know it's no big deal.

➥ **Going by how you feel, not by what the weighing scales say.** Weighing yourself can be really helpful and important, but I don't base my whole life around it anymore. If I'm feeling strong, happy and healthy then I know I'm doing fine. I don't chase numbers on the weighing scales.

➥ **Being consistent.** I realise that what often got me into bad eating cycles were extreme inconsistencies. I would starve and then overeat and then starve, and so on and so on. I now try not to have those extremes and be more consistent with my diet and lifestyle.

➥ **Controlling your environment.** If there are sweets and chocolate around the house then it becomes so hard not to eat them. So I now keep them out of easy reach. I might have the odd bit of chocolate in my car, and that's OK. Part of telling my parents the extent of my problem was for them to help me with what food was in the house.

➥ **Enjoying your eating.** I consciously try to enjoy my meals. I take my time to eat, being more mindful and grateful for how good the food is. I'll then make a statement at the end of a meal about how good it was and how full I am. That statement can really help me mentally accept that the meal is over.

I might outwardly give the impression that I get everything perfectly right with my diet because of how my body looks, but that is just not the case. The reality is that many people have difficult relationships with food and I hope that by sharing my experience it will help others.

In the last part of this chapter I want to focus on what I consider to be the right diet on a daily basis. I believe this is applicable to anyone but particularly people following this gymnastics journey with me.

The first and most important part is your attitude towards food. I have an attitude that I 'eat to train'. I am fuelling myself in order to train in the gym, and that should be no different from someone going to work for the day or whatever else they might be doing. Understanding that you are fuelling yourself is really important. I see far too many people carry an attitude of 'training to eat'. They regard training as a way of deserving food afterwards, which is not a healthy way to look at things. It can lead you towards that vicious cycle of under and overeating. Instead, see food as fuel – just a very enjoyable and tasty way of feeding your body what it needs to function well. As I have already stressed, I feel strongly about measuring progress rather than perfection. Having an occasional 'cheat', or 'treat' meal, or 'a little bit of something naughty' is an acceptable part of the progress. If we expect perfection from ourselves every day it can put so much pressure on the situation that it has the opposite effect.

So whatever you eat, here are my two important things to remember about diet:

➥ **Protein is really important**. We need to feed our bodies with protein in order to allow our muscles to recover properly from hard training. This is the same for both men and women. I think there is sometimes a misconception with women that protein will make their bodies very muscly, which some don't want, but this isn't necessarily true. If you take into account the amount of upper body exercises I do and the protein I eat, then I should be the size of a body builder! This is down to the balanced training that gymnastics gives you. It spreads the strength around your body and gives you a balanced look. Protein won't upset this; it will help it. I aim to have a good amount of protein in every meal, whether it is eggs, fish, meat or milk.

➥ **Long-lasting carbohydrates such as brown rice and bread are really helpful**. This is especially true if I'm doing double training sessions in a day, and will also be really important to people facing a long day at work or school. These foods can help me not to feel hungry throughout a day so I can steer clear from that under/overeating habit. Carbohydrates are the ultimate energy fuel so I don't eat any after 7.00 pm because I am generally inactive then, so they are not needed. That's when I would switch back to more protein-based foods. In general terms, most of my meals take up this composition: 45 per cent carbohydrate, 45 per cent protein and 10 per cent fat.

Four

Love the Journey

If any of you subscribe to my YouTube channel you will have heard me say many times that we have to 'love the journey'. I want to explain what that really means because it is something that gymnastics has taught me, and is absolutely vital to my progress as a person and an athlete.

Winning an Olympic bronze medal in Rio in 2016 was the biggest achievement of my life up to that point, and I learnt so many lessons from it, but none more so than when I got home. I look back on that period and call it an 'Oh my God!' moment.

I had trained for sixteen years to compete at a world level and winning the bronze was in some ways the crowning glory of that. Of course, it wasn't and isn't the end of my ambitions, but it was nevertheless a huge moment for me. The intensity of the occasion and the subsequent emotions were like nothing I had ever experienced before. But after I'd been home for a week or so, I felt completely flat. I looked at my medal and didn't really feel anything. Actually, that's not true – I felt sad.

Everything I thought made me happy in reality didn't truly do that. It was a strange feeling. Winning the bronze had brought me tears of joy but afterwards I didn't really feel any connection of happiness to it.

In those weeks after the Games I really struggled for motivation. I realised that I had defined my happiness in life on winning medals; and yet here I was looking at this piece of metal and not feeling anything.

Slowly but surely, the penny started to drop. I watched and listened to a lot of successful people talk and started to pull together how I was feeling. I began to reach my 'Oh my God!' moment. It wasn't an easy time but I'm now really grateful for the experience as it has helped me grow so much.

Suddenly I understood that I had defined my happiness by the end result, in this case a bronze medal. So once I had achieved it, there was nothing left to make me feel happy or motivated – just a gaping hole in my life.

I realised that I needed to reconnect to what it was all about for me: the journey – the time from when I was a kid obsessed with trying to learn to do a handstand and looking forward to every training session so I could try to master a new skill. That is what had made me happy and was why I had fallen in love with gymnastics.

I had completely fallen out of 'the moment' because I pinned so much on that big achievement. In my mind, the moment had come and gone in Rio. What I had forgotten was that there was a magical moment in every day and in every training session. I had moved away from being in the present; I had forgotten to 'love the journey'.

Once I came to terms with this, I moved forward as a person and an athlete. I now focus on the journey and enjoy every moment of it. The end result will take care of itself and, of course, I want that to be World and Olympic gold medals, but I don't let that pull me away from enjoying the process. And, most importantly, I don't define my happiness by that end result.

The end result doesn't have to be a medal. It can be buying a car or a house, or whatever else it might be that you are hoping to achieve. Once you reach that goal, you can rightly feel a huge sense of achievement, but don't define your happiness by it – otherwise you have nowhere to go after that. One of my goals is to one day drive a Ferrari, but I know it won't ultimately make me feel truly happy, and neither will an Olympic gold medal. It will be what I am doing with my life to achieve those goals that will define my happiness.

Nowadays, everything for me is about the process and being in the moment, and when I feel myself moving away from that, I pull myself back into it.

In some ways I see this realisation in my life as being 'humility vs ego'. Humility gives me the ability to want to learn and work every day, and to enjoy the moment I am in. Ego wants to take me off and tell me how wonderful I was in the past or will be in the future, the end result being that I sleepwalk through the present.

I now push away thoughts like 'I must win', 'What if that person does that?' or 'What will that person think of me?'

I absorb myself in the moment and love the process that I am in.

This has made me a better gymnast and the Commonwealth Games was a good example of that. In the all-around final I didn't lead the competition until I landed my high bar routine on the final piece. Up to that point I had been behind, but it was all process, process, process for me – enjoying what I was doing and concentrating on that moment I was in. I was focusing on the first bit of skill I needed to perform on that piece, then the second and so on. When one piece of apparatus was done, it was gone and I would enjoy the walk around in the rotation to the next piece. Then it was on to the next apparatus and the same process started again. It was fun!

Of course, I recognised that the final high bar routine in the all-around final was to decide the gold medal and it was a big moment, but the same things applied. Be in the moment, do the process I have done a million times and the rest will take care of itself...

PA Images.

'Loving the journey' is one of my most important life mantras now, but I believe it applies to us all.

Being out of the moment means we can be awake but asleep; ask yourself during any day if you are guilty of this. Do you go to work on Monday and have your mind on what happened at the weekend, or what you're going to do after work, rather than actually 'being' at work? Imagine how productive you could be if you were 100 per cent focused on what you wanted to achieve at 9.00 am on that Monday morning. You could probably accomplish more by lunchtime than some people do in a whole day.

This is why setting yourself daily goals is so important. It keeps you focused, but like all things with the mind, it needs training and practice. Remind yourself of how the journey is all-important and not hyperfocus on the end result. It will take care of itself if you are focused on enjoying what you are doing at that time.

There's no question that enjoying what you do makes this so much easier, and I would urge everyone to find work that they are passionate about. I appreciate it is not always as simple as that, but search for it and allow it to be part of your process towards happiness and success.

However, let's not forget that we are all human and it's impossible to stay in the moment all the time. Of course, I find myself getting caught up with 'What ifs' and 'Why did that happen?' In fact, some of that is healthy. Doing a quick review of a performance allows you to learn to replicate or improve it. But being consumed by this for too long can have an unhealthy effect. So when I slip out of the moment for too long, I try to quickly reset the balance.

The best example of this I can give is when I do my routines in training and competition. I use a 'six breaths' method. I take six deep breaths before I start any routine and listen to them, counting in-between each one. While I'm doing that I become aware of my surroundings – the weight of my feet on the floor, how my body feels, the temperature in the gym and so on. I get myself in the moment and it gives me clarity of thought on the process I need to go through: first skill, then second skill, then third, until the routine is finished.

You can use similar techniques when at work or even just enjoying a weekend. Become aware of your surroundings and this will immediately bring you back into the present.

Loving the journey is so important to me and it is a valuable lesson that gymnastics gave me. It is actually something I have managed to express on my YouTube channel. The content I put out is all about the journey. In January 2017, I had about 15,000 subscribers and by the end of the year it was around 650,000, which in YouTube terms is very fast growth. Yet

for most of this calendar year I was injured. So the content I was putting out that was being enjoyed by people wasn't based on the end result of a medal, because I was injured; it was all about the moments within my journey. That tells its own story.

This whole way of thinking extends throughout my family. My parents and sister are all in the same place – loving life, loving each other, staying in the moment and enjoying the experience. They do not measure my success by medals; it's measured on how we live our lives and how much we enjoy the journey.

As you can probably tell by now, I am very passionate about this! I wish for everyone to embrace it in their own lives. Gymnastics teaches you wonderful life lessons along the way and this is one of the most important.

Five

Get Ready for the 21-day Challenge

Over the next few chapters I am going to take you through a 21-day challenge, which will improve your overall physical strength and mobility. This challenge is suitable for everyone, regardless of what stage of fitness you are at. The exercises we will be doing sit right at the heart of why gymnastics is an incredible sport to improve your overall body functionality and balance.

After these twenty-one days I am very confident you will see improvement in your physical and mental wellbeing. You will also have a body management programme that you can take forward with you to maintain all the gains you have made.

I have purposely structured this challenge so there is the potential for progression throughout. Like I always say, I truly believe that gymnastics can change your life, and this is the start!

I also want to explain why we are doing what we are doing, and the significance of certain sections.

I am going to take this back to when I was fifteen years old and I suffered a double stress fracture in my lower back – the L5 in my lumbar spine, to be precise. It was obviously a huge shock at the time and I needed rest and rehabilitation, but the experience taught me some really good lessons about what I needed to do with my body going forward.

The reason my back suffered this injury was, quite simply, that there was too much stress being placed on it. This was partly a technical thing but mainly a body function thing. I needed my core and legs to be stronger and work better to give more support to my back. It was the first time in my life that I started to really understand how we need our whole body to work in balance. Of course, we will naturally have slightly stronger areas than others depending on what we do. For example, in proportion my shoulders are far stronger than my legs because of the nature of gymnastics. Likewise, a tennis player's hitting shoulder will be bigger than the other shoulder. But the key is that I can't just neglect the weaker parts of my body, otherwise too much stress is placed on the areas where most force is going through and I get injured.

A gymnast's physique is a beautiful thing. We look, for the most part, very much in balance. I believe that is because we are constantly working to manage the balance of our strength and movements through exercises every day. And guess what… you will be doing the same! It will improve your physique and, significantly, do it in a healthy way.

An important part of the 21-day challenge involves flexibility. Often when I speak to non-gymnast friends about stretching, the main response I get is that it is boring, uncomfortable and a bit of a hassle. Rarely do people realise that flexibility is such a vital part of your physical and mental wellbeing. A lad wanting to get muscly at the gym isn't interested in stretching because he can't see immediate benefits from it (like his muscles getting bigger!), but he's missing a big trick.

I want to change people's attitude towards flexibility. I honestly believe that embracing flexibility and mobility exercises can be an absolute game changer for people. It

activates your body and mind. You can be excited to do the exercises knowing that afterwards you will feel amazing.

We will go through specific exercises to help you learn how to do and develop a handstand. So, you might ask, why on earth do I need to learn how to do a handstand to improve my physical and mental wellbeing? The truth is that the handstand is an absolute fundamental of developing your body and mind through gymnastics. If I added up the amount of time I had been in a handstand since I was five, it would be a scary total. I may have been in a handstand more times than some people have been to the gym! I'm actually upside down at some point during virtually every day of my life now.

Learning to do a handstand will bring you confidence, strength, excitement and a sense of achievement. Earlier in the book I briefly listed the number of body parts that are working during a handstand – it truly is a full-body workout. But doing, or learning to do, a handstand involves huge amounts of focus and concentration. I am obviously very used to being in a handstand, but I couldn't close my eyes for a long period of time while in that position. It is a gymnastic position that works the body and mind simultaneously, and that's why it is so important. The handstand is the 'bread and butter' of gymnastics, and without it you can't progress.

To master a handstand requires persistence. As a kid all I wanted to do was learn how to do a handstand. I would be continuously kicking up into position and seeing how long I could hold it for. I remember being on holiday in Ireland with the family and there were fifteen of us sitting around watching a film in the lounge, and all I was doing was kicking up into a handstand. Can you imagine how mad I drove them? In the end, they used to just let me crack on with it. I was obsessed with how long I could hold a handstand for: it became two seconds, then five, then ten… and eventually I was able to walk around on my hands. This book talks about having a positive mindset and setting goals, and learning to do a handstand is a brilliant way of doing this. I just can't emphasise enough why doing exercises to learn and develop a handstand within this 21-day challenge is so important.

So 'chat time' is nearly over, but before we start working I want to take you through the twenty-one days and the exercises involved. It is all very simple, but it's worth familiarising yourself with the schedule, warm-up and each section's physical exercises before you start.

Six

Weekly Schedule

Monday	Tuesday	Wednesday	Thursday	Friday	Saturday	Sunday
Cardio	Handstand	Mindset	Full Body	Core	Flexibility	Rest

- ➡ The same 7-day pattern will follow for the full twenty-one days.
- ➡ It will challenge both your mind and body, and put you into a healthy routine to take forwards.
- ➡ We will progress the difficulty each week (other than flexibility). However, this is less important than just getting you into a good routine.
- ➡ The flexibility session will be repeated each week, but you will probably find you are able to progress your range as time goes on.
- ➡ This can ALL be done at home.
- ➡ Each daily session is approximately thirty minutes in total so is designed to fit within your day.

WARM-UP

It's essential that before each physical session you do a warm-up. This doesn't need to be extensive, but you definitely need to spend 5–10 minutes warming up.

Below are my top ten warm-up exercises along with photos and descriptions of how to do them. Please choose a few of them each time to do your warm-up. It would be good for you to go through all of them at least once during the twenty-one days.

Body squats

This is the starting position. Arms out at a 90-degree angle.

Use your legs to control yourself lowering down. Keep your knees pointing straight out and your back straight.

Arm circles (forward and back)

This is the starting position.

Above and overleaf: This is just showing the range of movement. You are making circles with your arms, keeping your arms straight. Try to get as much shoulder range as you can and keep your trunk as still as possible while you rotate your arms.

Neck side-to-side

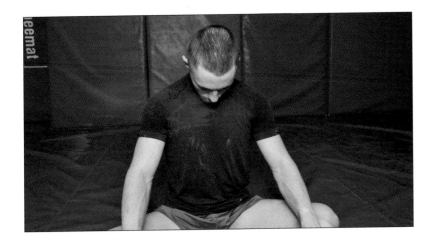

This is self-explanatory from the images. Take your time and don't go too vigorously.

Front support side rocks

This is the starting position, which is the front support.

Lean over each hand and shoulder as per the images.

Alternate hand-to-foot standing swings

This is the starting position. Arms straight out to the side, legs straight and bent at the hips.

Rotate so opposite hand goes to opposite foot. The goal is to keep your legs straight, but if this is too challenging then you can keep your knees slightly bent.

Trunk twists

This is the starting position. Stand up straight, with your legs slightly apart and your arms out to the side.

Rotate the trunk, keeping your hips forward. Stay in control.

Side leg swings

This is the starting position. Use a wall if you need to for balance.

Swing alternate legs out sideways, across your body. Keep your legs straight and body still.

Front-to-back leg swings

This is the starting position. Use a wall for your balance if you need to.

Keep your body in a straight line and keep both legs straight. Swing alternate legs forward and back so you create a 90-degree angle from your hips. Go as far as you can and keep everything in control.

Butt kicks

This is effectively jogging on the spot, with hands on your bum. The goal is to kick your heels onto your hands. Keep your chest up and body straight, and be light on your toes.

Jumping jacks

This is the starting position.

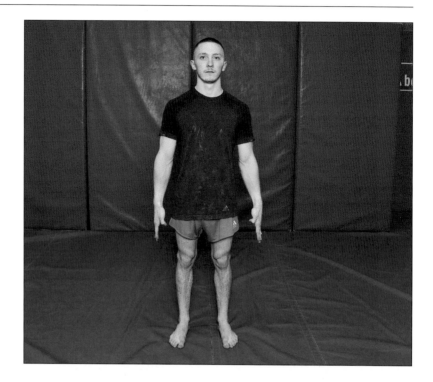

Jump and stretch your arms and legs out and then jump back into the starting position. Repeat as many times as you need to.

CARDIO EXERCISES

Burpee (with and without jump)

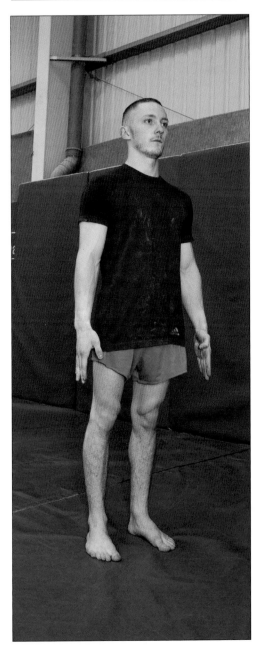 

This is the starting position.

From the standing position, bend down and put your hands on the floor in front of you.

Then push your legs back as you go into a front support position.

Finally, drive your legs forward and jump up into a straight position and repeat.

Alternate leg lunges

This is the starting position.

Step forward with alternate legs. Hips and knees should be at a 90-degree angle, keeping the back as straight as possible and eyes looking forward. We want our knees to be pointing straight forward and not leaning in or out of the straight line. It's important we keep that control in our knee.

Floor sprints

This is the starting position, which is the front support.

Bring alternate knees into your chest, almost like running. A great stability exercise through your shoulders and hands.

High knee running

Jogging on the spot and hands out, slap knees into your hands. Keep your chest up and back straight, and drive your knees into your hands.

Squat jump (with and without jump)

This is the starting position, with feet pointing slightly outwards and arms out at a 90-degree angle.

This is the same as normal squats, but just driving into a jump. Stay in control of your movement.

HANDSTAND EXERCISES

Wall stand back against

Stand as flat against the wall as you possibly can. Push the lower back into the wall. This is more challenging than people believe!

Tucked handstand on chair (static and walk)

This is the static version. Adopt a tucked position on the chair, at nearly a 90-degree angle and put pressure on your shoulders and hands.

This is the walkout version. Walk your hands out into the front support raise position, continuing to activate your core throughout.

Plank (normal and extended)

This is the normal plank. Elbows into the floor, straight line on your back.

This is the extended plank, where you are pushing your elbows out further and putting more pressure on your core.

Caterpillar walks

This is the starting position, which is a downward dog.

Walk out to the front support position…

Then reverse it back. This is a great exercise for stability and core strength.

Front support (with and without shrugs)

Your body wants to be in a completely flat position from feet to shoulders, with bum not too high or low. It is similar to the plank and you are activating your core. Shrug your shoulders in this position and then release. Keep this all under control.

Dish

The goal is to hide your ears with your arms. Really push your lower back into the floor. It is one of the best core exercises.

Candlestick

Aim to have your body as straight as possible with your hands on the floor. Keep your hips flat. If you're a beginner, you might not look as straight as possible but just aim for my position.

FULL BODY EXERCISES

Skater (with and without jump)

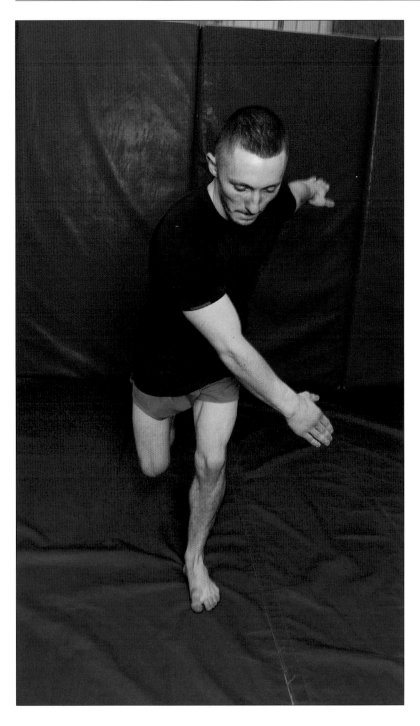

This is the starting position, starting on one leg.

Then slide across to the other leg as a skater would do and jump up with a high knee.

Alternate hand-to-foot

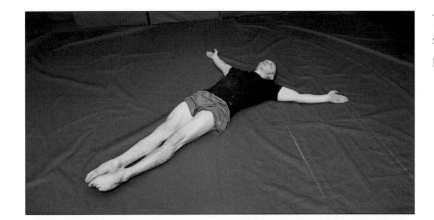

This is the starting position.

As per alternate hand-to-foot standing, rotate so you are moving opposite hand to opposite foot. Concentrate on squeezing your lower back into the floor and contracting your stomach muscles and core while making the movement.

Wide arm push-ups

This is the starting position, with a 90-degree angle from shoulder to elbow.

Lower your chest to the floor and then drive through your chest until your arms are straight again. Keep repeating.

Bulgarian squats (alternate legs)

This is the starting position, with back leg raised on a sofa or chair.

It is really important that the front knee is pointing straight forwards and not leaning to one side or the other. The goal is to get your hips at a 90-degree angle to your knee, keeping your chest up, back straight, arms down and hips square.

Full crunch

This is the starting position. Arms down and feet flat into the floor.

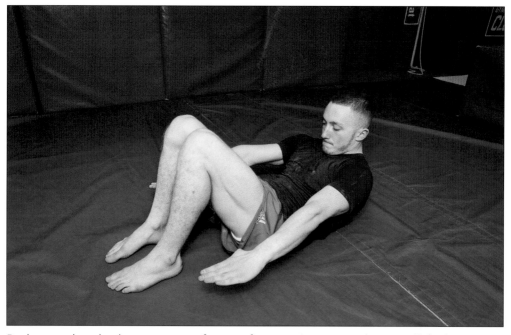

Push your hands down to your feet as far as you can, and you will feel a strong contraction in your stomach muscles.

Front support shoulder taps

This is the starting position, which is the front support.

Move your opposite hand to opposite shoulder in a controlled fashion and squeeze your core while doing it.

Arch swimmers on your front

This is the starting position.

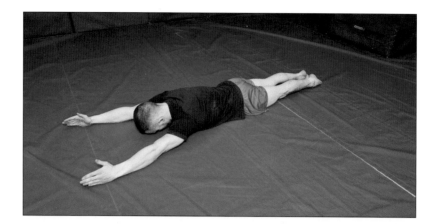

Start with your forehead on the floor, lifting your opposite arm and leg and moving them simultaneously up and down. Try keeping your arms and legs straight.

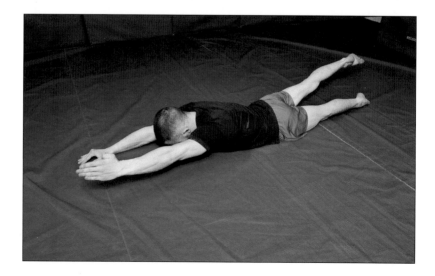

CORE EXERCISES

Some of these exercises are repeated from the handstand exercises, but that is simply because they are very important!

Front support (normal and legs raised)

This is the starting position, which is the front support.

The same technique as normal front support but with your feet raised. It makes it more challenging, with more pressure on your shoulders and core.

Bridge raises

This is the starting position. Feet flat on the floor with knees pointing towards the ceiling. Hands flat on the floor.

Push your hips up towards the ceiling, aiming for a flat line from your knee to your shoulder.

Bicycles

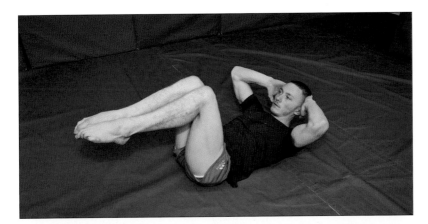

This is the starting position. Both hands on the back of the head, knees up, and legs making a 90-degree angle.

Leg straight out simultaneously with opposite knee to opposite elbow. The goal is to keep your lower back pressed against the floor and go at your own pace.

Leg lowers

This is the starting position.

Take your legs down as close to the floor as possible, but don't touch the floor. Pull them back up to a 90-degree angle. Keep lower back squeezed into the floor.

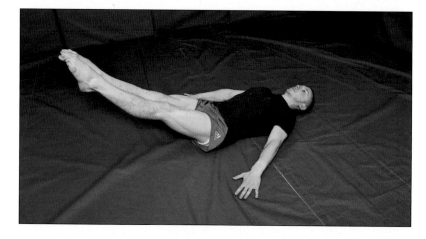

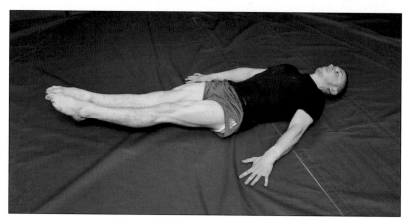

Dish roll to arch

This is the starting position. Hiding your ears with your shoulders, your upper and lower half are off the floor and push your lower back into the floor.

It's really important to keep your arms and feet off the floor when rolling, and then roll to either side.

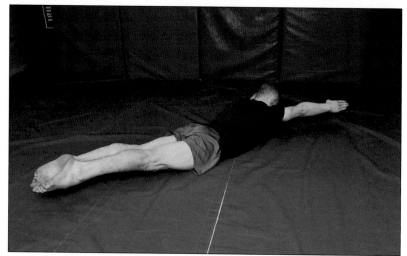

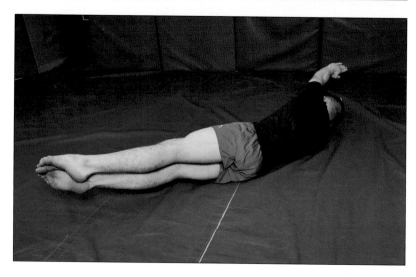

This is the finishing position.

Candlestick

Plank rotations

Start in the
plank position.

Opposite arm
and point
elbow to the
ceiling. Rotate
to the side
plank position
and then back
into normal
plank position.

FLEXIBILITY AND MOBILITY EXERCISES

Neck movements

Arm rotations (forward and back)

Lower back stretches

This is the starting position. Use your hands to support you and stretch your side and lower back.

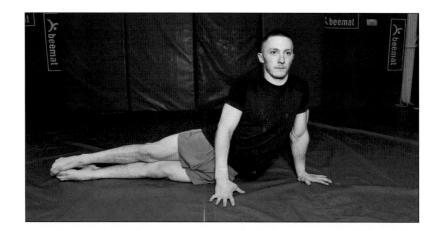

Push up with your hands from this position. Go to where is comfortable for you.

Bring your feet over the head, but only if this feels comfortable for you. Do not go beyond your natural stretch be careful with this if you find it too challenging.

Straddle sit up and down (forward and back)

This is the starting position.

Stretch forward with your arms and endeavour to go as low as you can, keeping your legs straight and your knees on the floor. Obviously, the aim is to get your chest on the floor, but just go as far as is comfortable for you.

Straddle sit side-to-side

This is the starting position.

The goal is opposite hand to opposite foot, but we are trying to put the hand behind your head and hide your ear. It's important we use the full stretch through your lower back and sides, but just go as far as is comfortable for you.

Squat sit to standing pike

This is the starting position.

Getting your nose onto your knees is your goal, but go as far as you can. Put your hand flat on the floor and keep your legs straight.

Downward dog to arch support

This is the starting position. Aim to have a 90-degree angle from your feet to your hands, i.e. through your hips. Push tall through your shoulders and keep your legs straight.

Bend through to the arch, looking towards the ceiling. It gives a great stretch through the lower back.

Arms/shoulders static

Pull your arm across your chest and pull back with the other arm. Go as far as is comfortable for you.

Pike fold

Extend
your legs
straight out,
endeavouring
to put your
nose on
your knees.
If it is too
challenging,
then just go as
far as you can.

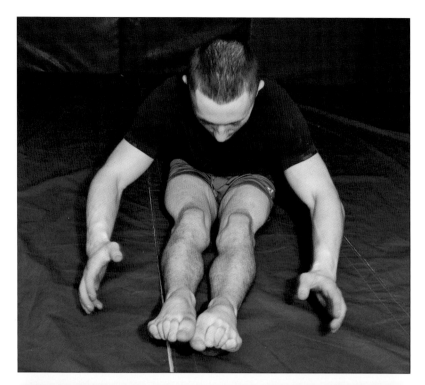

Shoulder splits

Start on your knees with both hands on the floor in the wide arm position and take one arm out straight. Rotate and it will create a great stretch through your pectorals and shoulders.

Impingement stretch (each arm)

This is the starting position. Shoulder tucked into body and arm going out at a 90-degree angle.

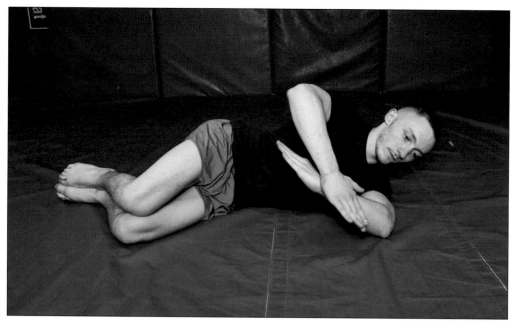

Push your hand as close to the floor as possible and you will feel an incredible stretch through the back of the shoulder. Repeat on each arm.

Standing pectoral stretch (wall, each arm)

Put your hand flat against a wall and rotate around to feel the stretch in the pectorals and biceps.

Seated quad stretch (each leg)

Start in the straddle position and lift one knee up and place your foot across the other leg, as per the image. Then rotate and place your opposite elbow across the knee to create a stretch in your lower back. Repeat on the other side.

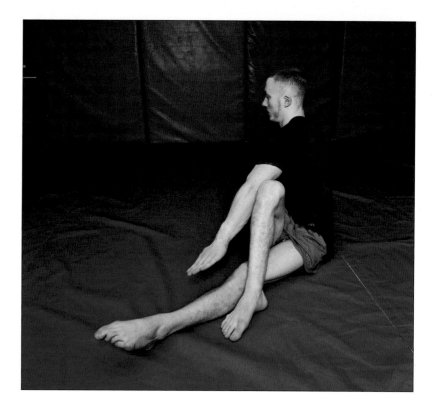

Seated lower back rotation (each side)

As with the seated quad stretch, sit in the straddle position, tuck the lower part of your leg in and get a great stretch in your quad. The more you lean back the more intense the stretch.

Seal stretch

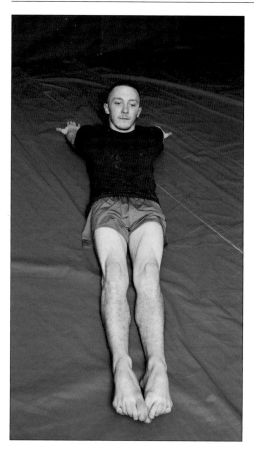 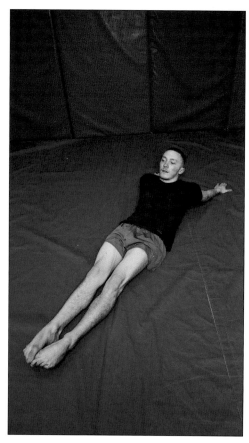

Lay back and push your arms behind you, as per the image. This picture is extreme because of my flexibility, so just go as far as you can. Keep your body straight.

SO ENOUGH CHAT... LET'S GET TO WORK!

Seven

21-day Challenge: Week 1

Monday	Tuesday	Wednesday	Thursday	Friday	Saturday	Sunday
Cardio	Handstand	Mindset	Full Body	Core	Flexibility	Rest

MONDAY, CARDIO

Warm-up:	5–10 minutes
Main session:	3 sets of each exercise
Set 1:	30 seconds work, 30 seconds rest
Set 2:	40 seconds work, 20 seconds rest
Set 3:	50 seconds work, 10 seconds rest

1 minute rest in between each set (if needed)

Cardio Exercises

❶ Squat jump

❷ Burpee without jump

❹ High knee running

❸ Floor sprints

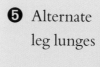

❺ Alternate leg lunges

TUESDAY, HANDSTAND

Warm-up: 5–10 minutes

Main session: 2 sets (no rest between sets)

30 seconds on each exercise

30 seconds rest in between each exercise

❶ Wall stand back against

❷ Tucked handstand on chair (static)

❸ Plank (normal)

❹ Front support (without shrugs)

❺ Dish

❻ Caterpillar walks

❼ Candlestick

WEDNESDAY, MINDSET

Topic – 'Attitude'

Our attitude to life and everything that goes with it is a choice. I believe that how we deal with life is 90 per cent attitude and 10 per cent fact. So it isn't the actual event (fact) that is taking place, but the attitude we choose to adopt in dealing with it.

You choose your inner dialogue, your self-talk, and, therefore, essentially how you react to any given situation.

Let's expand on the example I gave in Chapter 2.

You're on your way to work and you immediately get stuck in a massive traffic jam. You have a choice right then and there. You can moan and complain about your luck and how this has ruined your day, with your head consumed with negative self-talk: 'Why does this always happen to me?' 'I'm going to have the worst day', *or* you can choose a different attitude and be very aware of your self-talk. It can be positive: 'I'll take this moment to ring my mum', 'I'll put some amazing music on the radio', 'I'll take this time to plan out my day'. You can choose how you react to every situation that you encounter during a day. It doesn't mean you will love every situation that you have to deal with, but how you react to it is *your* choice.

So my challenge for you from this session is just to be mindful of how you are reacting to situations throughout your day. What is your self-talk/inner dialogue like? Is it positive or negative? If you take real note of this then you have won half the battle. When we become fully aware of our behaviour and attitude, we then have the ability to change it. Choose the attitude you want and help yourself be happy throughout the day.

THURSDAY, FULL BODY

Warm-up: 5–10 minutes
Main session: 2 sets (1 minute rest in between each set)

30 seconds rest in between each exercise

❷ Alternate hand-to-
foot –10 on each

❸ Wide arm push-
ups – 15 reps

❹ Bulgarian squats
(alternate legs) –
10 on each leg

❺ Full crunch – 15 reps

❶ Skater (without
jump) – 10 on
each leg

❻ Front support shoulder taps –
15 on each

❼ Arch swimmers on your front –
15 on each

FRIDAY, CORE

Warm-up: 5–10 minutes
Main session:

30 seconds on each exercise
60 seconds rest in between each exercise

❶ Leg lowers

❷ Front support (normal and legs raised)

❸ Bridge raises

❹ Bicycles

❺ Plank rotations

❻ Dish roll to arch

❼ Candlestick

SATURDAY, FLEXBILITY

Warm-up: 5–10 minutes
Main session:

❶ Neck rolls each
way – 30 seconds

❷ Arm rotations, front
and back – 30 seconds

❸ Squat sit to standing
pike – 30 seconds

❹ Straddle sit up and
down – 30 seconds

❺ Straddle sit side-to-
side – 30 seconds

❻ Lower back stretches
– 30 seconds

❼ Downward dog to arch support – 30 seconds

8 Shoulder splits – 90 seconds

9 Arms/shoulders static – 5 minutes

10 Pike fold – 5 minutes

11 Seated lower back rotation – 45 seconds each side

13 Seal stretch – 90 seconds

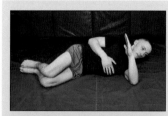

14 Impingement stretch – 45 seconds each arm

12 Standing pectoral stretch (wall) – 45 seconds each arm

15 Seated quad stretch – 45 seconds each leg

SUNDAY, REST

Although Sunday is a rest day, I would like you to use it as a day to plan your nutrition for the week. Good nutrition does require planning.

List your meals for the week and your food shopping accordingly. If you plan it well on the Sunday then you won't rush for food throughout the week. Rushing often leads to under and overeating as we forget to eat properly and then overeat when we are starving.

Use this day to put in place a balanced nutrition schedule for the week.

Eight

21-day Challenge: Week 2

Monday	Tuesday	Wednesday	Thursday	Friday	Saturday	Sunday
Cardio	Handstand	Mindset	Full Body	Core	Flexibility	Rest

MONDAY, CARDIO

Warm-up:	5–10 minutes
Main session	
(as per Week 1):	3 sets of each exercise
Set 1:	30 seconds work, 30 seconds rest
Set 2:	40 seconds work, 20 seconds rest
Set 3:	50 seconds work, 10 seconds rest

1 minute rest in between each set

Cardio Exercises

❶ Squat jump

❷ Burpee without jump

❹ High knee running

❸ Floor sprints

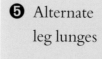 ❺ Alternate leg lunges

TUESDAY, HANDSTAND

Warm-up: 5–10 minutes

Main session: 2 sets (no additional rest in-between sets)

45 seconds on each exercise

45 seconds rest in between each exercise

❶ Wall stand back against

❷ Tucked handstand on chair (static)

❹ Front support (with shrugs)

❸ Plank (extended)

❺ Dish

❻ Caterpillar walks

❼ Candlestick

WEDNESDAY, MINDSET

Topic – 'Loving the Journey'

Earlier in the book I described what I meant by 'loving the journey'. I came back from the 2016 Rio Olympics with a bronze medal, but afterwards really struggled for motivation and actually felt very down. I quickly realised that I had focused all my life on the physical achievement, i.e. the medal, but that actually wasn't what made me happy. My happiness lay with the process of winning that medal – the training every day, the obsession to improve a skill and basically my absolute love of gymnastics. I was in love with the process and not the end result. That was just the icing on the cake.

So I went back to focusing on the process and enjoying it every day. My motivation and love for training returned, and I carry them forward into my competitions now. This translates into every walk of life. If you are happy and in love with what you are doing, you are going to get the results.

So my challenge for you in this session is to write down the answers to the following questions:

- ➥ Are you passionate about what you are doing for work?
- ➥ If yes, then why are you passionate about it? Really focus on your 'why'.
- ➥ If no, then what can you change? Or where can you find passion in something else you love, e.g. a hobby?

Keep these answers and always refer back to them. You can write them up on the wall or keep them in an envelope in a draw, but always look back at them.

THURSDAY, FULL BODY

Warm-up: 5–10 minutes
Main session: 2 sets (1 minute rest in between each set)

30 seconds rest in between each exercise

❶ Skater (without jump) – 10 on each leg

❷ Alternate hand-to-foot –10 on each

❹ Bulgarian squats (alternate legs) – 10 on each leg

❸ Wide arm push-ups – 15 reps

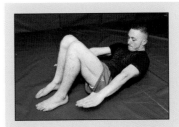

❺ Full crunch – 20 reps

❻ Front support shoulder taps – 20 on each

❼ Arch swimmers on your front – 20 on each

FRIDAY, CORE

Warm-up: 5–10 minutes
Main session:

30 seconds on each exercise
30 seconds rest in between each exercise

❶ Leg lowers

❷ Front support (normal and legs raised)

❸ Bridge raises

❹ Bicycles

❺ Plank rotations

❻ Dish roll to arch

❼ Candlestick

SATURDAY, FLEXBILITY

Warm-up: 5–10 minutes
Main session:

❶ Neck rolls each way – 30 seconds

❷ Arm rotations, front and back – 30 seconds

❸ Squat sit to standing pike – 30 seconds

❹ Straddle sit up and down – 30 seconds

❺ Straddle sit side-to-side – 30 seconds

❻ Lower back stretches – 30 seconds

❼ Downward dog to arch support – 30 seconds

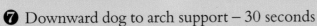

❽ Shoulder splits – 90 seconds

❾ Arms/shoulders static – 5 minutes

❿ Pike fold – 5 minutes

⓫ Seated lower back rotation – 45 seconds each side

⓭ Seal stretch – 90 seconds

⓮ Impingement stretch – 45 seconds each arm

⓬ Standing pectoral stretch (wall) – 45 seconds each arm

⓯ Seated quad stretch – 45 seconds each leg

SUNDAY, REST

As per last Sunday, use this day to plan out your nutrition schedule for the week.

Nine

21-day Challenge: Week 3

Monday	Tuesday	Wednesday	Thursday	Friday	Saturday	Sunday
Cardio	Handstand	Mindset	Full Body	Core	Flexibility	Rest

MONDAY, CARDIO

Warm-up:	5–10 minutes
Main session:	3 sets of each exercise:
Set 1:	30 seconds work, 30 seconds rest
Set 2:	40 seconds work, 20 seconds rest
Set 3:	50 seconds work, 10 seconds rest

1 minute rest in between each set

Cardio exercises

❶ Squat jump

❷ Burpee with jump

❹ High knee running

❸ Floor sprints

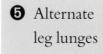 ❺ Alternate
        leg lunges

TUESDAY, HANDSTAND

Warm-up: 5–10 minutes

Main session: 2 sets (no additional rest in between sets)

60 seconds on each exercise

30 seconds rest in between each exercise

❶ Wall stand back against

❷ Tucked handstand on chair (walk)

❸ Plank (extended)

❹ Front support (with shrugs)

❺ Dish

❻ Caterpillar walks

❼ Candlestick

WEDNESDAY, MINDSET

Topic – 'Gratitude'

Today we are talking about a very simple thing that can change your life – gratitude.

Everyone has something they should be grateful for. I believe we should all be grateful to be alive! I'm just grateful to be a human being and for having the opportunity to live the best life I can.

It is impossible to be negative and grateful at the same time, and that is such an important point. Let's appreciate and understand what gratitude can do for your life. It improves your mindset and general attitude for each day.

So my challenge for you in this session is to go away and write down a Gratitude List.

Write down everything you can be grateful for in your life and keep that list near you. Look back at it when you're feeling negative or down. You can also constantly update your Gratitude List. Rewriting it every two or four weeks is a really good idea. It is something that is really important to me.

THURSDAY, FULL BODY

Warm-up: 5–10 minutes
Main session: 2 sets (30 seconds rest in between each set)

20 seconds rest in between each exercise

❶ Skater (without jump) – 10 on each leg

❷ Alternate hand-to-foot –10 on each

❹ Bulgarian squats (alternate legs) – 15 on each leg

❸ Wide arm push-ups – 15 reps

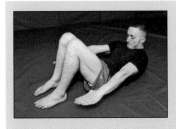

❺ Full crunch – 20 reps

❻ Front support shoulder taps – 20 on each

❼ Arch swimmers on your front – 20 on each

FRIDAY, CORE

Warm-up: 5–10 minutes
Main session:

45 seconds on each exercise
30 seconds rest in between each exercise

❶ Leg lowers

❷ Front support (normal and legs raised)

❸ Bridge raises

❹ Bicycles   ❺ Plank rotations

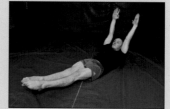

❻ Dish roll to arch

❼ Candlestick

SATURDAY, FLEXBILITY

Warm-up: 5–10 minutes
Main session:

❶ Neck rolls each way – 30 seconds

❷ Arm rotations, front and back – 30 seconds

❸ Squat sit to standing pike – 30 seconds

❹ Straddle sit up and down – 30 seconds

❺ Straddle sit side-to-side – 30 seconds

❻ Lower back stretches – 30 seconds

❼ Downward dog to arch support – 30 seconds

8 Shoulder splits – 90 seconds

9 Arms/shoulders static – 5 minutes

10 Pike fold – 5 minutes

11 Seated lower back rotation – 45 seconds each side

13 Seal stretch – 90 seconds

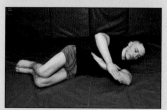

14 Impingement stretch – 45 seconds each arm

12 Standing pectoral stretch (wall) – 45 seconds each arm

15 Seated quad stretch – 45 seconds each leg

SUNDAY, REST

We did it! Now that wasn't so bad, was it?

I'm hoping that by now you've got into an excellent routine and are feeling the benefits both in mind and body. These twenty-one days are not designed to break you with something so punishing that you would never take it forward. It's all about getting into and maintaining good habits.

I hope you are now in a place where you have a routine that you are confident to continue with. There are, of course, many more progressions you can make, some of which I will follow up in future books – but for now, you have the basis to use gymnastics to genuinely change your life for the better.

Well done Team!

Ten

So, Where to From Here?

My aim at the start of this book was to convince you that gymnastics can genuinely change your life. I really hope I have achieved that.

Gymnastics is beautiful and unique, and can do so much for your body and mind. It has taught me so many life lessons that have helped me progress as a person and I'm sure it will continue to do so for more years to come. I hope I have brought these lessons to life for you, including my past relationship with food. It was important for me to be honest about this, because I wanted to make it clear that despite the level at which I compete, I am just as fallible as the next person.

I hope you have given the 21-day challenge a real go and can already feel the benefits from it. It is a great platform from which to develop good habits that you can take forward and progress at whatever pace you want.

However... if you have tried the 21-day challenge and don't think the physical aspect of gymnastics is for you, then I still hope you take away some of the principles about mindset and attitude I have talked about. I believe they are so important to find happiness and meaning in your life.

Whatever you do, find something you are passionate about and love the journey. Practise your positive self-talk and choose the attitude you want to adopt in life. Measure yourself against the progress you are making towards your goals and dreams, and not against the perfect scenario, which is unlikely to lead to perfection. Plus your journey will change as you change and develop. Any setbacks are merely kinks in the road towards achieving what you are truly capable of. It's all there for the taking, if you want it enough!

I will leave you with a quote from Simone Biles, speaking after she won four Olympic gold medals at Rio in 2016. This is what it is all about:

> *Surround yourself with the dreamers, the doers, the believers and the thinkers; but most of all surround yourself with those who see greatness within you, even when you don't see it yourself.*

Remember… train smart, keep it real!

Nile x